ESSENTIAL

CAKES

ESSENTIAL TIPS

CAKES

Barbara Maher

DORLING KINDERSLEY

London • New York • Stuttgart • Moscow

A DORLING KINDERSLEY BOOK

Editor Alexa Stace
Art Editor Ann Burnham
DTP Designer Robert Campbell
Series Editor Gillian Roberts
Series Art Editor Clive Hayball
Production Controller Lauren Britton

Recipes and techniques for Tips 21, 23, 41, 64, 67, 77, 78, 86, 90, 94, 95 by Anne Willan.
Recipes and techniques for Tips 40, 46, 63, 84, 101 copyright © 1991 Dorling Kindersley and
The Hearst Corporation. Reprinted from The Good Housekeeping Illustrated Book of Desserts
by arrangement with William Morrow & Company, Inc., a division of The Hearst Corporation.

**Follow either metric or imperial units throughout a recipe, never a mixture
of the two, since they are not exact equivalents.**

**Raw eggs can transmit salmonella. Avoid serving recipes containing
raw eggs to the elderly, young children, and pregnant women.**

First published in Great Britain in 1997 by
Dorling Kindersley Limited,
9 Henrietta Street, London WC2E 8PS

Visit us on the World Wide Web at http://www.dk.com

Copyright © 1997 Dorling Kindersley Limited, London

A CIP catalogue record for this book is available from the British Library

ISBN 0-7513-0423-9

Text film output by The Right Type, Great Britain
Reproduced by Colourscan, Singapore
Printed and bound by Graphicom, Italy

ESSENTIAL TIPS

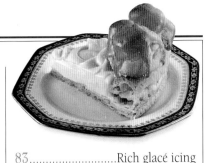

BASIC TOOLS & EQUIPMENT

1 TINS & UTENSILS

Pictured on these two pages is a selection of the most useful equipment for making cakes. Accurate kitchen scales are also essential for successful baking.

◁ *Measuring spoons* help to measure accurately.

▽ *Serrated knife* slices cakes into even layers.

▽ *Citrus zester* can remove fine strips of peel without pith.

△ *Rubber spatula* cleanly scrapes out the mixing bowl.

△ *Balloon whisk*, for egg whites and cream, gives more volume and allows better control than an electric beater.

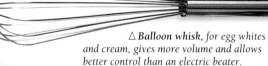

△ *Nylon piping bags* can be washed to use time and again, and are available in many sizes.

△ *Small nozzles* to pipe decorations in chocolate and icing ensure good results.

△ *Large nozzles* are needed to pipe choux pastry, meringue, and whipped cream.

△ *Gugelhupf tin* is patterned to mould an attractive shape.

△ *Sandwich tins* to bake sponge-cake layers can be loose bottomed.

Angel food tin ▷ has a central tube and deep sloping sides: it must be spotless and not greased for the cake to rise and reach full height.

▽ *Springform tin* has a spring clip and loose bottom that make it easier to release and turn out the cake.

▽ *Shallow tins* & flat baking sheets are ideal for Swiss rolls and meringues.

2 LINING A ROUND TIN

Preparing a cake tin helps to prevent the cake sticking, making it easier to remove. The tin is first greased, then lined with non-stick silicone paper. Rich fruit cakes also need extra protection (*Tip 5*).

1 △ Brush the inside of the tin evenly with melted butter. Cut one strip of paper to fit the sides, ends overlapping slightly, making sure it is 5cm (2in) wider than the depth of the tin.

2 △ Fold in one long edge of the paper strip by 2.5cm (1in) and crease well. Unfold, then make angled cuts at 2.5cm (1in) intervals along this long edge, up to the folded line but not beyond it.

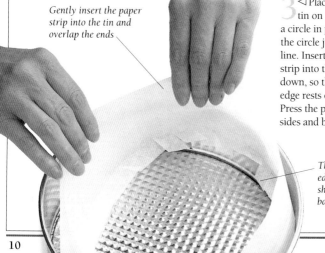

Gently insert the paper strip into the tin and overlap the ends

3 ◁ Place the base of the tin on paper and draw a circle in pencil. Cut out the circle just inside the line. Insert the long paper strip into the tin cut-side down, so that the creased edge rests on the base. Press the paper on to the sides and base of the tin.

The cut, folded edge of the strip should rest on the base of the tin

4 △ Lay the paper circle on the base of the tin, smoothing it out so that the cut edge of the strip lies flat underneath. Make sure the overlapping join of the strip lies flat: use a bit more butter if necessary. If using greaseproof paper, brush once more with melted butter.

Quality Bakeware
When buying tins, choose the best quality you can afford. Thin metal tins (a poor investment) let cakes burn in the oven, and may prevent even rising.

Size of Tin
Always use the size stated in the recipe. Also check the tin's depth. If the cake is in too deep a tin, it will not rise well; if too shallow, the mixture will run over.

Unusually Shaped Tins
These can't be lined with paper. Grease twice with butter, dust with flour, then shake out the excess.

3 LINING A LOAF TIN

Square or rectangular tins should also be lined, to make sure the cake turns out with no trouble.

1 △ Place the tin on a rectangular sheet of paper and draw around the base in pencil. Crease along the lines to the paper's edges. From the longer sides, cut along the creases to the pencil lines.

2 △ Grease the tin. Fold up the sides of the rectangle and drop into the tin, tucking the flaps behind the longer sides. Press on to the base and sides.

11

4 DOUBLE-LINING A CAKE TIN

Rich mixtures that need long and slow baking should have a double thickness of paper on the base to protect them from the heat. With heavy fruit cakes that are baked for a long time, it is also advisable to have thick paper wrapped around the outside of the tin (*Tip 5*).

1 △ Fold a square of paper in 4, then in triangular eighths. With the point at the tin's centre, cut level with the edge.

2 △ Cut a second circle in the same way. Cut a strip longer and deeper than the sides. Grease the tin and place one circle in the base. Grease the paper.

3 △ Fold and cut the strip (*Tip 2*) then press around sides so folded edge overlaps base. Place second circle in base to hold down overlap. Grease.

5 EXTRA PROTECTION

Line the tin as above. Fold a sheet of brown paper into a strip the same depth as the tin and slightly longer around. Wrap it around the outside and then secure with string. Place the tin on a baking sheet lined with brown paper.

PROTECT FRUIT CAKES WITH A WRAPPING

INGREDIENTS & TECHNIQUES

6 TAKING CARE

When baking, it is important to use the exact ingredients specified in the recipe. Try to use the best quality available, and do not store dry goods too long, as they will soon deteriorate.

Icing sugar

Eggs

Flour

Light & dark muscovado sugar

7 SIFTING FLOUR

Sift the flour twice through a fine sieve. This aerates the flour and improves the texture of the cake. Sift again with any other dry ingredients to mix them in evenly.

TAP THE SIEVE WITH YOUR PALM

8 SEPARATING EGGS

Crack the shell gently on the edge of a bowl. Separate the shell and pour the yolk from one half into the other without breaking it, letting the white fall into the bowl.

KEEP THE YOLK INTACT

9 ZESTING FRUIT

Lemon, orange, or lime zest is often used to flavour cakes. Rub the skin of scrubbed or unwaxed fruit over the finest side of a grater: take care not to remove any of the bitter white pith underneath. For longer strands of zest to decorate cakes, use a citrus zester (*Tip 1*).

USE SCRUBBED OR UNWAXED FRUIT

10 SUGAR SYRUP

For syrup, dissolve 500g (1lb) sugar in 150ml (¼ pint) cold water. Add a pinch cream of tartar mixed with1 tsp water. Bring to the boil, then remove from heat. For "soft ball", boil to 115°C/240°F on a sugar thermometer; for caramel, boil until it reaches 173°C/345°F.

DO NOT STIR THE SUGAR SYRUP

11 WHIPPING CREAM

Pour the chilled cream into a bowl, and use a balloon whisk to whip the cream until it just forms soft, floppy peaks. If you want to pipe the cream, whip until it forms stiffer peaks, but do not overbeat or the cream will curdle.

DOES FAT CONTENT MATTER?
Cream for whipping needs to have a fat content of at least 30 per cent. When you want to pipe decorations that must hold their shape, a richer cream with at least 40 per cent fat is the most satisfactory.

WHIP UNTIL SOFT PEAKS TURN OVER AT ENDS

12 DISSOLVING GELATINE

Gelatine has to be softened in cold water and then dissolved over heat before using. Cool before adding to a mixture or strings will form. Use 1 teaspoon gelatine powder to 1 tablespoon liquid.

AN ALTERNATIVE
Agar-agar (made from seaweed) can be used instead of gelatine (which is made from beef) if you are vegetarian.

1 △ Sprinkle gelatine over cold liquid and leave for 5 minutes.

2 ◁ Place bowl over hot water until liquid is clear, then leave to cool.

13 ROASTING HAZELNUTS

Hazelnuts give a wonderful flavour to cakes, but the skin can be hard to remove. The nuts must first be roasted, then rubbed in a cloth.

1 ▷ Roast on a baking sheet at 180°C/ 350°F/gas 4 for 15 minutes, until the skins are lightly brown and flaking off.

2 △ Tip the nuts onto a tea towel. Fold the cloth over, and then rub the nuts gently in it to remove the skins. Cool.

14 TESTING FOR DONENESS

Sponges should be well risen, golden, and just starting to shrink from the sides. The top will spring back when pressed gently with a finger. Test any cake by inserting a fine skewer into the centre. If the cake is done, the skewer will come out clean. If still sticky, bake for another 5 minutes.

TEST IN THE CENTRE WITH A SKEWER

15 TURNING OUT & COOLING

Leave to rest in the tin for a few minutes, run a palette knife around the sides and turn out on to a wire rack. With springform tins, release the clip and lift away the sides. To remove a loose-bottomed base, turn cake on to a wire rack and slide a palette knife between the base and the cake. Gently peel off the paper and leave to cool.

PROTECT YOUR HANDS WITH A CLOTH

16 STORING & FREEZING

Cakes must be well wrapped to prevent them from drying out. Wrap all undecorated cakes in greaseproof paper, then foil, and store in an airtight container. A layered cake filled with cream or chocolate is best stored in a large airtight plastic box and kept in the refrigerator. To freeze, wrap the cake in greaseproof paper or foil and place in a freezer bag. Freeze layered or decorated cakes in a rigid container. Defrost in a cool place, or in the refrigerator.

17 BAKING KNOW-HOW

Follow these rules for success. If problems do occur, just consult the box below for the probable cause.

- Have eggs at room temperature.
- Bake for the minimum time specified before opening the oven door.
- Stagger cake layers on oven shelves: don't place them one above the other.
- If the cake browns too quickly, loosely cover the top with a layer of foil.

TESTING WITH A FINGER

Problem	Explanation
Cake has dense, heavy texture	Whisked cakes: insufficient air whisked into egg and sugar mixture; flour not folded in gently. Creamed cakes: butter, sugar, and eggs not beaten long enough; too much flour added; flour blended in too vigorously.
Creamed mixture curdled	Ingredients not at room temperature; butter and sugar not creamed sufficiently before eggs added; eggs added too quickly, not beaten in gradually one by one.
Dried fruit sunk to the bottom	Pieces of fruit too large and heavy; sticky glacé fruit not washed and dried; fruit not dusted with flour before adding to mixture.
Cake sunk in the middle	Oven temperature too hot, so cake not cooked through for long enough; oven door opened too soon, creating draught.
Swiss roll cracked	Sponge overcooked and too dry; mixture not spread evenly in tin; sponge left too long before rolling up.
Cake peaked and cracked	Oven temperature too hot, causing outside of cake to form crust too quickly; cake on too high a shelf in oven.
Fruit cake overcooked and top burned	Fruit cakes require longer baking; cover top with foil half-way through cooking. If using fan-assisted oven, set lower temperature.

18 CAKE VARIETIES

Whether a simple sponge or an elaborately layered confection, there is a cake to suit almost every occasion. Increase your repertoire by mastering the techniques that ensure perfect baking results.

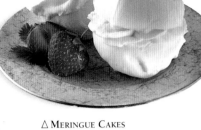

△ MERINGUE CAKES
Filled with fruit, whipped cream, or even both, meringue cakes are light in texture, yet taste luscious and rich.

△ CHEESECAKES
Cheesecakes can be baked, or set with gelatine and chilled, or moulded. (Note that uncooked cakes may contain raw eggs.) With each type, the texture is always soft and moist.

△ LAYER CAKES
A whisked or creamed sponge, or a nut mixture can be used for layer cakes. Chilling the finished cake lets the layers settle.

◁ LITTLE CAKES
Choux puffs are a delicious mouthful, and much easier to make than they look.

DECORATIONS ▷
A simple cake looks so impressive
and tastes extra special when it's
decorated with sugar-frosted fruit.
You can prepare it and leave to
dry a few hours before using.

△ FRUIT CAKES
Traditional fruit cakes are rich,
heavy, and packed with succulent
dried and glacé fruits. More glacé
fruits sparkle like jewels on top.

▽ CHOCOLATE CAKES
Learn the right way to handle
chocolate, and you'll have few
problems – even
with the most
elaborate cakes.

▽ TOPPINGS & FILLINGS
Toppings such as butter cream can
also be fillings. Others, like sugar
paste, make a good base for piping.

△ WHISKED CAKES
Whisked cakes – Swiss rolls and roulades
(rolled cakes), fatless sponges, and angel
food cakes – have a light, delicate texture,
and can be filled with whipped cream or
soft icing. Plain angel food cake is lovely
served with fresh fruit compote for dessert.

WHISKED CAKES

19 LIGHT & AIRY

Whisking is one of the basic methods of cake-making – ideal for producing light, fatless sponges, angel cakes, and Swiss rolls. Whisked cakes have a fine, delicate texture, which is achieved by beating in as much air as possible. In some recipes, the egg yolks and whites may be whisked separately.

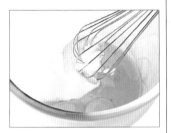

USE FRESH EGGS & FINE SUGAR

20 PERFECT MIXTURE FOR A FINE CAKE

It is essential to beat the eggs and sugar until pale, creamy, and thick enough to leave a ribbon trail on the surface when the beater is lifted. Use either a balloon whisk or a hand-held electric beater.

1 Whisk the eggs and sugar in a large bowl to the "ribbon" stage. The mixture should be thick, pale, creamy, and leave a clear trail on the surface that lasts for 4 seconds.

2 Stir in 2 tablespoons of the egg whites, if whisked separately. Sift the flour into the bowl and fold gently into the mixture, using a large metal spoon.

3 Add the remaining egg whites, if whisked separately, folding them in gently until evenly mixed. Do not overwork. The mixture should be smooth, light, and airy.

21 GENOESE CAKE

Makes 8 slices

Ingredients

125g (4oz) plain flour
pinch of salt
4 eggs
135g (4oz) caster sugar
½ tsp vanilla extract
60g (2oz) unsalted butter, melted and cooled
1½ recipe quantities coffee butter cream (Tip 71)
flaked almonds

TO DECORATE

Press flaked almonds on the sides. Score top with fine lines. Pipe butter cream swirls around edge. Put flaked almonds in between.

1 Grease and line a 22cm (8½in) round cake tin. Preheat the oven to 180°C/350°F/gas 4. Sift the flour and salt together twice, to aerate well.
2 Whisk the eggs and sugar to the ribbon stage (*Tip 20*). Whisk in the vanilla. Sift on and lightly fold in the flour in thirds. With the last, add the cooled melted butter (leave its sediment behind).
3 Pour into the cake tin. Bake in the preheated oven for 35 minutes, or until a skewer inserted into the centre comes out clean. Allow to cool in the tin for 5 minutes. Turn out onto a wire rack. Leave to cool thoroughly before proceeding.
4 Cut the cake into 3 layers and sandwich layers with some of the coffee butter cream. Cover top and sides with remaining butter cream (*Tip 72*).

22 SWISS ROLL

Use a Genoese cake mixture (*Tip 21*), and bake in a 36 x 24cm (14 x 10in) rectangular tin for 20 minutes only. Jam, cream, butter cream, or chocolate ganache are all good fillings, and the roll may be decorated on the outside as well.

For a jam filling (as below), ideally fill and roll the cake while warm. For cream fillings, the cake needs to be covered with silicone paper, then a slightly damp tea towel, and left to cool in its tin before being turned out, filled, and rolled up.

1 △ Remove the cake from the oven and turn out while still hot on to a sheet of greaseproof or silicone paper sprinkled with caster sugar.

3 ▽ Using a large palette knife, spread the filling in an even layer over the warm cake.

2 △ Release the paper lining at one corner and slowly peel off, being careful not to tear the delicate sponge, especially at the edges. The cake is now ready to be filled and rolled.

Spread the filling to within 1cm (½in) of the edge of the cake.

4 △ Neatly trim away 1cm (½in) from each edge. Use the back of a knife to score a shallow line 5cm (2in) from the edge of one short end. With the scored end facing you, lift up the edge of the paper and use it to help roll up the cake as tightly as possible. Cool on a rack, seam-side down.

DECORATION
A dusting of icing sugar contrasts nicely with the jam filling.

23 ANGEL FOOD CAKE

Makes at least 8 generous slices

Ingredients
90g (3oz) plain flour
30g (1oz) cornflour
300g (10oz) caster sugar
375ml (12fl oz) egg whites (about 12)
1½ tsp cream of tartar
pinch of salt
½ tsp vanilla extract
frosting and chopped nuts, to decorate

1 Preheat oven to 180°C/350°F/gas 4. Sift flour and cornflour, add a third of the sugar, and sift twice.
2 Whisk egg whites, add cream of tartar and salt, and beat until stiff. Gradually whisk in rest of sugar, then whisk until mixture is glossy and holds peaks. Add vanilla and fold in flour in 3 stages.
3 Spoon into ungreased tube tin and bake for 40–45 minutes. Place tin upside down on rack to cool. Decorate with frosting and nuts.

CAKE HAS A VERY DELICATE TEXTURE

23

CREAMED CAKES

24 RICH & BUTTERY

The creamed butter sponge is another basic cake that lends itself to innumerable variations. Its texture is moist and slightly close. Use a large bowl and a hand-held electric mixer, if possible, to incorporate as much air as you can while beating. The most well-known type of creamed sponge is the Victoria sandwich (*Tip 28*), often served filled with jam and cream and lightly dusted with icing sugar to finish.

A WOODEN SPOON CAN ALSO BE USED

25 BASIC METHOD

To achieve the right texture, the butter, sugar, and eggs must be mixed vigorously together to beat in air. This is known as "creaming". If you use a wooden spoon, you'll need patience and a strong arm.

1 Beat the butter for a minute or two until soft and creamy. Add the sugar and go on beating hard for 3–5 minutes, until pale and fluffy.

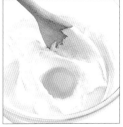

2 Add the eggs one at a time, beating well between each addition. The mixture will slacken, then thicken when ready for the next egg.

3 If the mixture curdles when adding the eggs, it will hold less air. To prevent this, sift in a spoonful of flour when beating in the last 2 eggs.

26 ADDING SIFTED FLOUR

When you add the flour, try to do so very lightly. This will help to retain the air that gives the finished cake its light texture. Sift the flour twice, then fold it in with a metal spoon. Stirring or beating the mixture will simply knock the added air out of it.

1 Spoon the sifted flour into a sieve. Hold up over the bowl and sift again into the mixture.

2 Gently cut and fold the twice-sifted flour into the creamed mixture using a large metal spoon.

27 WHISKING EGG WHITES

BEAT UNTIL SOFT PEAKS FORM

If whisking egg whites to fold into a cake mixture, take care not to whisk them too stiffly – they will not blend in evenly, making the cake look patchy. Always use a spotlessly clean bowl, and a balloon whisk or electric mixer. Whisk slowly until foamy, then beat faster – but still with caution.

28 VICTORIA SANDWICH

Preheat oven to 180°C/350°F/gas 4. Grease, flour, and line 2 x 20cm (8in) sandwich tins. Beat 250g (8oz) butter and 250g (8oz) caster sugar until pale and fluffy. Beat in 4 eggs one at a time. Sift 250g (8oz) self-raising flour over mixture and fold in. Divide between tins and bake for 25 minutes until golden brown and springy to the touch. Turn out onto a wire rack to cool.

29 SURE SUCCESS

Have all the ingredients at room temperature before you start, and be sure to preheat the oven to the temperature specified in the recipe. Don't open the oven door until halfway through the baking time.

Mixture should just drop lazily from spoon

30 ALL-IN-ONE METHOD

This easy method combines the eggs, sugar, butter, and flour in one go. All the ingredients must be at room temperature. Beat in a large bowl until everything is well blended, and the mixture is smooth, thick, and creamy.

USE AN ELECTRIC FOOD MIXER

31 POUND CAKE

Makes 12–16 slices

Ingredients

125g (4oz) plain flour
125g (4oz) potato flour (from health food shops)
1 tsp baking powder
250g (8oz) butter
250g (8oz) caster sugar
seeds from ¼ vanilla pod
4 large eggs (size 1)
1 tsp grated lemon zest
1 tbsp milk
icing sugar, to decorate

1 Preheat the oven to 180°C/350°F/gas 4. Grease a 1.5 litre (2½ pint) Gugelhupf tin with melted butter twice, then dust with flour.
2 Sift the flour, potato flour, and baking powder together. Beat the butter, sugar, and vanilla seeds until pale and fluffy. Beat in the eggs one by one, adding a little of the flour if the mixture begins to curdle. Beat in the lemon zest.
3 Gradually beat in the flour until evenly mixed. Stir in the milk. Spoon the mixture into the tin and smooth level. Bake in the preheated oven for about 1 hour, or until a skewer inserted into the centre comes out clean (*Tip 14*).
4 Ease the cake away from the sides with a round-bladed knife. Leave to rest for 10 minutes.
5 Turn out onto a wire rack and leave to cool. Before serving, dust with a little sifted icing sugar.

PLAIN BUT GOOD
Pound cake is satisfyingly rich, with a firm crumb and a buttery flavour.

32 POUND CAKE VARIATIONS

Pound cake is easily made by the creamed technique (*Tip 25*). Although it is not elaborate, the addition of special ingredients such as chocolate, fresh fruit, or spices and nuts transforms the cake into a memorable treat. Decorate the cake with glacé icing (*Tip 81*) if liked.

△ **MARBLE CAKE**
Make basic mixture, minus the milk. Spoon half into another bowl. Blend 2 tbsp rum, 75g (2½oz) melted chocolate, and 2 tbsp cocoa and stir into one half. Drop alternate spoonfuls of plain and chocolate mixture into tin and bake for 1 hour.

△ **MIXED SPICE CAKE**
Sift 1 tsp cinnamon and ½ tsp grated nutmeg with the flour. Make the mixture, folding in 60g (2oz) chopped roasted hazelnuts (Tip 13). Bake for 1 hour. Dust with sifted icing sugar.

FRESH FRUIT CAKE ▷
Make the mixture, minus the milk. Mix 375g (12oz) chopped apricots, plums, or peaches with 1 tbsp lemon juice and fold in with the flour. Bake for 1¼ hours.

FRUIT CAKES

33 RICH & HEAVY

Many fruit cakes are made by the creaming method (*Tip 25*). In these cakes, the batter mostly acts only as a binder for the other ingredients. Careful baking is vital. Heavy fruit cakes can take 2 hours or even longer, and therefore the temperature must be kept low.

TEXTURE IS DENSE BUT STILL MOIST

34 PREPARATION

Advance preparation ensures the best result. Be sure to double-line the tin and use a paper wrapping as well (*Tip 5*). Fresh nuts are a must (those stored for some time can become rancid). Rinse the dried fruit and wash glacé fruit well in warm water to get rid of the sticky sugared coating. Dry all the fruit thoroughly on kitchen paper, then toss with a little of the recipe flour until lightly coated.

△ PECAN NUTS

△ GLACÉ FRUITS   △ DRIED FRUITS

35 AVOID PROBLEMS

If the cake starts to brown too quickly, cover loosely with foil. Test for doneness in the usual way by inserting a fine skewer into the centre: it should come out clean. Let the cake cool thoroughly in its tin before turning out onto a rack.

36 STORING FRUIT CAKES

Store rich fruit cakes for at least 1 month before eating. This allows the flavour to mature and develop. Wrap in greaseproof paper, or in muslin moistened with brandy, and place in an airtight container.

37 BRANDIED FRUIT CAKE

Makes 24 slices

Ingredients

375g (12oz) bread flour
1 tbsp baking powder
400ml (14fl oz) water
175g (6oz) butter, cut up
375g (12oz) caster sugar
175g (6oz) dried apricots,
quartered
375g (12oz) sultanas
125g (4oz) glacé cherries
60g (2oz) glacé pineapple
6 tbsp brandy
3 eggs, lightly beaten
finely grated zest of
1 orange and 1 lemon
Decoration
4 tbsp marmalade
60g (2oz) each natural and
red glacé cherries, halved
60g (2oz) angelica, cut into
diamonds
125g (4oz) glacé pineapple
125g (4oz) pecan nut
halves

1 Preheat the oven to 160°C/
325°F/gas 3. Grease and double-
line a deep square 20cm (8in) tin.
2 Sift flour and baking powder twice. Bring
water, butter, sugar, apricots, and sultanas to
the boil over low heat. Boil for 20 minutes.
3 Cool the boiled mixture, then pour into a
bowl and add the chopped glacé fruit and the
brandy. Beat in the eggs and orange and lemon
zest. Add the flour and beat until evenly mixed.
4 Spoon into the tin and level the surface. Bake
for 2 hours, or until a skewer comes out clean.
Cool in the tin on a wire rack, then turn out.
5 Warm the marmalade and use to brush top of
cake. Arrange the fruit and nuts over the cake,
then brush with the remaining marmalade.

*Marmalade gives a
glossy finish*

LAYER CAKES

38 PERFECT PRESENTATION

Layer cakes can be made with whisked, creamed, or ground nut mixtures. It's essential to have even layers of cake and filling for a neat presentation, so allow yourself plenty of time to assemble elaborate cakes. Chilling the finished cake for 4–5 hours allows the layers to settle.

MAKE THE LAYERS EVEN

39 CUTTING, ASSEMBLING, & FILLING LAYERS

To form layers, bake several thin cakes or, alternatively, slice a single thick cake horizontally into two, three, or four layers. Whipped cream, butter cream, jam, and fresh fruit are the most popular fillings.

1 Place the cake on a firm surface. Rest one hand lightly on the cake to hold it steady. To cut in half, slice horizontally through the centre with a sharp serrated knife. Cut even layers by measuring and marking all around the cake with toothpicks before slicing into layers.

2 Starting with the top, carefully separate the layers by sliding the thin base of a loose-bottomed flan tin between each of them. When each layer is supported, lift off and set to one side. Moisten each layer by lightly brushing its top with sugar syrup (*Tip 10*) or liqueur.

3 Have the filling soft enough to spread and not pull up crumbs. Use a metal spatula to spread the chosen filling evenly to within 5mm (¼in) of the edge. Cover with the second layer and gently press down. Repeat with each layer, then even up the edges when finished.

40 LATTICE-TOP CAPPUCCINO CAKE
Serves 8

Ingredients
5 eggs, separated
165g (5¼oz) icing sugar,
  sifted to remove lumps
45g (¾oz) cocoa powder,
  sifted, plus extra
  for sprinkling
150ml (¼ pint) double
  or whipping cream
250g (8oz) full-fat soft
  cheese, softened
30g (1oz) plain chocolate,
  coarsely grated
2 recipe quantities coffee
  butter cream (Tip 71)
chocolate-covered coffee
  beans or chocolate beans,
  to decorate

ASSEMBLING THE CAKE
*Place bottom cake layer
on a plate. Spread with
half the filling. Repeat
the layering, finishing
with a top layer of cake.*

TO DECORATE
*Spread three-quarters
of butter cream over
top and sides of cake.
Spoon rest in piping
bag with star nozzle.
Pipe lattice top and
border. Put a coffee
bean in each diamond.*

1 Preheat oven to 200°C/400°F/gas 6. Grease a 33 x 23cm (13 x 9in) Swiss roll tin; line with non-stick baking parchment.
2 Beat egg whites in a large bowl until soft peaks form. Gradually add 60g (2oz) icing sugar, beating until whites stand in stiff peaks.
3 Beat egg yolks until thick, then beat in 60g (2oz) icing sugar, and cocoa. Fold in egg-white mixture one-third at a time with a metal spoon.
4 Spoon mixture into tin and spread level. Bake for 15 minutes or until cake feels springy to the touch. Turn out onto a clean tea towel sprinkled with cocoa. Peel off lining paper; leave to cool.
5 Whip cream until stiff peaks form. Beat rest of icing sugar into softened cheese. Stir in grated chocolate, then fold in cream. Chill filling.
6 Cut cake crossways into 3 equal pieces. Trim the crisp edges with a sharp knife.

41 BLACK FOREST CAKE
Makes 8–10 slices

TO SERVE
*Cut in slices with
a sharp knife.*

Ingredients
*3–4 slices dark rye bread
60g (2oz) plain chocolate,
chopped
60g (2oz) plain flour
½ tsp baking powder
2 tbsp cocoa powder
4 eggs, separated
100g (3½oz) caster sugar
90g (3oz) ground almonds
1 tbsp Kirsch
1 tbsp water
75g (2½oz) melted butter,
cooled
125ml (4fl oz) sugar syrup
(Tip 10) mixed with
2 tbsp Kirsch
500ml (¾ pint) Chantilly
cream (Tip 94)
250g (8 oz) canned black
cherries, drained and
halved
60g (2oz) grated chocolate
10 cherries dipped in
chocolate (Tip 100)*

GETTING AHEAD
*The cake can be baked
up to 3 days ahead of the
day you need it. Leave it
unsliced and undecorated
and store in an airtight
container in a cool place.
Make the cherries dipped
in chocolate a day before.*

1 △ Preheat the oven to 180°C/350°F/gas 4. Line and grease a 20cm (8in) cake tin. Work the bread and chocolate in a food processor. Sift the flour, baking powder, and cocoa into a bowl. Mix in bread and chocolate. Beat egg yolks with half sugar until light and thick.

2 △ Stir almonds, Kirsch, and water into the yolks. Whisk egg whites until stiff, add remaining sugar, and whisk until glossy. Fold one-third whites into egg yolks. Fold flour mixture into yolks in 3 batches. Fold in rest of whites. Add the melted butter and fold in.

3 △ Pour mixture into cake tin and bake in preheated oven until top springs back when pressed lightly, about 35–40 minutes. Run knife around side of tin to loosen cake, then turn out onto a wire rack lined with silicone paper. Peel off lining paper and leave cake to cool.

4 △ Cut cake into 3 horizontal layers. Brush each layer with Kirsch syrup. Spread bottom layer with one-eighth of Chantilly cream and top with half the cherries. Spread with another eighth of cream. Add second cake layer and fill in same way. Place top layer cut side down.

5 △ Neaten the sides of the cake and smooth any cream that has pressed out. Spread half remaining cream over top and sides of cake. Placing cake on a stand with a plate underneath, press the grated chocolate around the sides, using a piece of silicone paper to help apply it.

6 △ Transfer cake to a serving plate. Mark a lattice pattern on top of the cake with the edge of a palette knife. Using a medium star nozzle, pipe the remaining cream around the top edge. Top each rosette with a cherry dipped in chocolate, and chill before serving.

MERINGUE CAKES

42 MAKING MERINGUES

Some classic cakes, such as vacherin and Pavlova, are based on meringue. It is made with whipped egg whites and caster sugar, baked at very low heat until crisp and dry, but still almost white. Plain meringue stores well for up to 2 months, enabling you to produce a cake in minutes.

USE A BALLOON WHISK

43 SIMPLE MERINGUES

Makes 10 individual meringues

Ingredients
2 egg whites
pinch of cream of tartar
125g (4oz) caster sugar, sifted
150ml (¼ pint) double cream
fresh strawberries, to decorate

DECORATE WITH FRESH FRUIT

1 Put the egg whites in a large, clean bowl and whisk slowly until they become thick and frothy. Add the cream of tartar then whisk more quickly until they form stiff peaks.
2 Gradually whisk in half the sugar, 1 tbsp at a time, until the mixture is glossy and stiff peaks form. Sift over the remaining sugar and gently fold in. (For a stiffer meringue for piping, whisk in the remaining sugar gradually.)

3 Preheat the oven to 120°C/250°F/gas ½. Spoon 10 large spoonfuls on to baking sheets lined with silicone paper, about 2cm (¾in) apart. Bake for 50–60 minutes until crisp and dry, then switch off the oven and leave until completely cold. Whip the cream until stiff and then use it to sandwich the meringues in pairs.

44 PIPING MERINGUES

Using a piping bag fitted with a 1cm (½ in) plain nozzle, pipe rounds in a spiral on a lined baking sheet. The underside of the baked meringues should sound hollow when lightly tapped with a finger.

PIPE FROM THE CENTRE OUTWARDS

45 SUMMER BERRY VACHERIN

Makes 10–12 slices

Ingredients
4 recipe quantities simple meringue (Tip 43)
granulated sugar
Filling
180g (6oz) crushed raspberries, mixed with 30g (1oz) caster sugar
180g (6oz) puréed strawberries, mixed with 30g (1oz) caster sugar
1.25 litres (2 pints) double cream, whipped with 30g (1oz) caster sugar & 6 tbsp Grand Marnier
assorted fresh fruit, to decorate

1 Preheat the oven to 110°C/225°F/gas ¼. Mark 22cm (8½ in) circles on 3 lined baking sheets. Spread half the meringue inside the circles. Pipe stars around the edges with a 1cm (½ in) nozzle, piping a double row of stars for the top disc.
2 Sprinkle with sugar and bake for 2½–3 hours until crisp and dry. Leave in the oven until cold.
3 Mix one-third cream into raspberries and one-third into strawberries. Sandwich discs with the two fruit creams, double star layer on top.

TO DECORATE
Spoon plain cream into top layer and cover with fresh fruit.

46 PAVLOVA
Makes 8 slices

Ingredients
3 egg whites
180g (6oz) caster sugar
1 tsp white vinegar
1 tsp cornflour
300ml (½ pint) whipping cream, whipped stiffly
5 kiwi fruit, thinly sliced

OTHER FRUIT TOPPINGS
Kiwi fruit is the classic topping for Pavlova, but you can also use halved strawberries, peeled and finely sliced nectarines or peaches, fresh or canned pieces of pineapple, or peeled and cubed papaya.

1 Preheat oven to 150°C/300°F/gas 2. Mark a 20cm (8in) circle on a lined baking sheet.
2 Beat egg whites in a large bowl until soft peaks form. Gradually sprinkle on the sugar, 1 tbsp at a time, beating well after each addition. Blend the vinegar and cornflour and whisk into the whites with the last of the sugar.
3 Spread the meringue inside the circle on the baking sheet, building up the edges higher than the centre. Place in centre of oven, reduce heat to 140°C/275°F/gas 1, and bake for 1 hour or until slightly coloured. Turn off oven and leave to cool completely.
4 Carefully remove Pavlova and place on a serving plate. Spoon two-thirds of cream into the meringue. Arrange most of the kiwi slices on top. Top with remaining cream and kiwi slices.

TO DECORATE
Arrange slices of kiwi fruit on top.

CHEESECAKES

47 SOFT & MOIST

The texture of cheesecakes can vary from fluffy and smooth to dense and rich, but each type is soft and rather moist. Traditional cheesecakes were baked, but now they are also set with gelatine and chilled, or moulded and chilled.

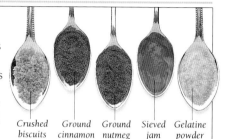

Crushed biscuits   *Ground cinnamon*   *Ground nutmeg*   *Sieved jam*   *Gelatine powder*

48 BAKED GOLDEN CHEESECAKE

Makes 10–12 slices

Ingredients

250g (8oz) sweet shortcrust pastry, defrosted if frozen
400g (14oz) curd cheese
125ml (4fl oz) soured cream
2 eggs, separated
1 egg yolk
125g (4oz) caster sugar
1 tbsp vanilla sugar
2 tsp lemon zest
60g (2oz) raisins, soaked in 2 tbsp dark rum
icing sugar, to decorate

1 Preheat the oven to 200°C/400°F/gas 6. Grease a 22cm (8½in) tin. Roll out half the pastry into a 23cm (9in) circle. Press on to the base and slightly up the sides. Prick with a fork, bake for 10–15 minutes, then leave to cool. Roll out rest of pastry and line the sides of the tin. Lower the heat to 180°C/350°F/gas 4.

2 Beat cheese, cream, yolks, sugars, and zest until thick. Whisk whites into soft peaks. Stir 2 spoonfuls into cheese then fold in remainder with raisins. Pour into tin and bake for 1 hour. Turn off oven and leave until cold.

TO SERVE
Unmould the cheesecake from tin when completely cold. Dust the top lightly with icing sugar to serve.

49 MANGO & PASSION FRUIT CHEESECAKE
Makes 10–12 slices

Ingredients
*180g (6oz) digestive
biscuits, crushed
½ tsp ground cinnamon
pinch of grated nutmeg
75g (2½oz) butter, melted
1 tbsp apricot jam, melted*
Filling
*425g (14oz) can mango
slices
1½ tbsp gelatine
7 passion fruit, halved
zest and juice of 1 orange
4 eggs, separated
150g (5oz) caster sugar
200g (7oz) mascarpone
200ml (7fl oz) double
cream, whipped
2 mangoes, sliced
1 kiwi fruit, sliced*

1 Grease a 22cm (8½ in) tin and line the base. Mix together the biscuits, spices, butter, and jam. Spoon into the base, press down evenly with a spoon, then chill.
2 Drain mangoes and place 90ml (3fl oz) juice in a heatproof bowl. Add gelatine and dissolve (*Tip 12*). Place 6 mango slices around sides of tin and chop remainder. Sieve pulp of 6 passion fruit and add the juice to the chopped mangoes. Stir in the gelatine with orange zest and juice.
3 Whisk egg yolks and sugar until thick and pale. Whisk in the mascarpone. Stir in the fruit mixture and leave until it starts to set.
4 Whisk egg whites to soft peaks. Fold cream into fruit mixture, then egg whites. Pour into tin and chill for at least 5 hours or until set.
5 Unmould and decorate with the sliced fruit. Spoon pulp of remaining passion fruit on top.

PLEASE NOTE
*Eggs are uncooked
in this cake.*

38

50 PASHKA

Makes 10–12 slices

Ingredients

250g (8oz) unsalted butter
180g (6oz) caster sugar
500g (1lb) curd cheese
2 egg yolks
125ml (4fl oz) double cream
3 drops vanilla extract
125g (4oz) raisins
60g (2oz) candied peel, chopped
2 tbsp chopped blanched pistachio nuts
125g (4oz) toasted almonds, chopped

To Decorate
Use 250g (8oz) mixed crystallized clementines, citron, pears, melon, and orange peel to decorate.

Please Note
This cake contains uncooked eggs.

1 Beat the butter and sugar until pale and fluffy. Beat in the curd cheese until smooth, followed by the egg yolks, one at a time. Stir in the cream and vanilla. Add the raisins, candied peel, nuts, and almonds, and stir to mix evenly.
2 Spoon into a clean flowerpot 14cm (5½ in) high and 15cm (6in) across the top, lined with damp muslin. Lift excess cloth over the top and tuck in around the edge. Fit a small plate inside the rim and place a heavy weight on top. Stand on a plate and chill for 6 hours, or overnight.
3 Invert the cake onto a plate. Carefully lift off the pot and peel off the muslin. Thinly slice the crystallized clementines and citron peel (*see box*) and arrange around base. Cut remaining fruit into diamonds and arrange in 4 crosses around the sides of the cake, with a smaller one on top.

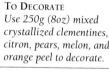

CHOCOLATE CAKES

51 CHOCOLATE ESSENTIALS

Working with chocolate needs care, but the techniques are quickly learned. Plain chocolate, with a high proportion of cocoa butter, is generally used for baking, as milk chocolate is harder to work with.

CHOP WITH A LARGE BROAD KNIFE

52 MELTING

Break the chocolate into pieces and place in a heatproof bowl. Set over a pan of barely simmering water and leave for 5 minutes.

Stir the melting chocolate now and then until smooth and glossy

54 TEMPERING

Tempering makes chocolate more malleable and shiny. Melt the chocolate and pour two-thirds on to a marble slab or work surface. Using a palette knife, spread back and forth for 3 minutes until it is almost set. Quickly return to bowl with remaining chocolate and reheat over hot water, stirring.

WORK THE CHOCOLATE BACK AND FORTH

53 IN TROUBLE?

If chocolate contacts water or steam, it tightens into a rough mass and will not melt. Stir in 1–2 tsp vegetable oil until smooth again.

55 CHOCOLATE DECORATIONS

For decorations, you can use either plain block chocolate or plain melted chocolate. Try to work in cool conditions. Keep your hands cool, and avoid handling the chocolate too much. Allow several hours for the decorations to harden properly before using. They can be stored in the freezer or refrigerator for 1–2 weeks.

△ **Heart** *is a very easy shape, made with melted chocolate.*

◁ **Lattice** *is piped free-hand in a lacy pattern.*

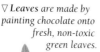

▽ **Leaves** *are made by painting chocolate onto fresh, non-toxic green leaves.*

△ **Ruffles** *are a finer version of the scrolls pictured below.*

Fleur-de-lis ▷ *uses melted chocolate carefully piped to shape.*

Daisy *has both white and dark chocolate for contrast.* ▷

△ **Scrolls** *are made by pushing a knife along the surface of chocolate.*

△ **Fruits dipped in chocolate** *are best if they're small with a stem: try either grapes or cherries.*

56 PIPING CHOCOLATE DECORATIONS

Draw or trace the shape onto a sheet of white paper. Place a sheet of silicone paper on top and fasten both papers to work surface with sticky tape. Leave shapes to dry at room temperature. Avoid handling once set.

TAKE GOOD CARE
Remove with a palette knife when firm, handling shapes as little as possible.

1 Make a greaseproof paper cone. Fill with melted chocolate. Fold over top to seal, then cut off tip with scissors.

2 Follow the outline of the drawing, letting the chocolate fall evenly from the tip without forcing it. Leave to set.

57 SCROLLS

Pour melted chocolate onto a flat surface and spread out evenly with a metal spatula. Leave to dry. Holding a large knife at an angle, push it along the surface so that the chocolate rolls up into long scrolls.

HOLD THE KNIFE AT A 45° ANGLE

58 CURLS

Make curls and shavings from a block of chocolate at room temperature. Holding the block at an angle, use a vegetable peeler to shave small curls off the edge of the block on to a plate.

MAKE FINE SHAVINGS OR LARGER CURLS

59 LEAVES

Use pliable leaves with deep veins, such as rose. Leave a little stem exposed.

NON-TOXIC LEAVES
Use rose, violet, or mint leaves, never azalea, ivy, mistletoe, or poinsettia.

1 With a small, clean paintbrush, coat the underside of each leaf with melted chocolate in a thin, even layer.

2 Leave to cool, then chill until set. Very carefully peel off leaves, touching the chocolate as little as possible.

60 BUTTERFLIES

Practise your drawing a few times first. Press firmly with a hard, sharp pencil as you draw the butterfly on the silicone paper so that its imprint will also come through onto the bottom half of the paper.

1 ◁ Cut rectangles of silicone paper, 10 x 6cm (4 x 2½ in) then fold crosswise in half. Draw outline of a butterfly on each folded rectangle, using centrefold for the body. Unfold paper and place on flat surface, tracing side down.

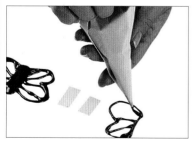

2 △ Tape paper drawings to work surface. Fill paper piping bag with melted chocolate and pipe over whole tracing, including down centrefold. Remove tape and lift off paper.

3 △ Place butterflies over bun tin tray or egg cartons so paper is slightly bent at centrefold. Refrigerate for 1 hour until set. Carefully peel off paper with cool hands.

61 CHOCOLATE GANACHE

Ganache is a rich, creamy chocolate mixture that is used to ice or fill cakes. Coffee or a liqueur is sometimes added to flavour the ganache. For a lighter texture, it can be whipped until fluffy.

1 Break 250g (8oz) plain chocolate into chunks, then chop as finely as possible with a large, heavy kitchen knife. Place the chocolate in a large bowl.

2 Heat 250ml (8fl oz) double cream until almost boiling, then pour over the chocolate. Stir until the chocolate has melted then allow to cool, stirring occasionally.

3 Add 1 tbsp liqueur to the mixture (if using) and stir until blended in. For a lighter texture, beat until fluffy, but be careful not to overbeat, or the ganache will be stiff.

62 CHOCOLATE GLAZE

This rich glaze is ideal for covering a moist chocolate cake. Place 175g (6oz) plain chocolate drops and 30g (1oz) butter in a heavy pan over very low heat and stir until melted (*Tip 52*) and smooth. Make sure the pan is a very heavy one, otherwise the chocolate will burn. Remove from the heat and beat in 3 tbsp milk and 2 tbsp golden syrup. Use while warm.

◁ **MAKE THE GLAZE**
Gently melt butter and chocolate in heavy-bottomed pan over low heat.

SPREAD THE GLAZE ▷
Dip a palette knife in hot water and use to spread the still-warm glaze evenly over the entire cake.

63 CHOCOLATE TRUFFLE CAKE

Makes 10 slices

Ingredients

325g (11oz) butter
750g (1½lb) plain chocolate, broken up
600ml (1 pint) water
3 eggs, beaten
400g (14oz) plain flour, sifted with 1¼ tsp baking powder
400g (14oz) caster sugar
300g (10oz) icing sugar
175ml (6fl oz) double cream

TO DECORATE
Grate 60g (2oz) chocolate and sprinkle around top of cake. Decorate with a rose.

1 Grease 3 round 23cm (9in) tins. Preheat oven to 160°C/325°F/gas 3. Place 250g (8oz) butter, 375g (12oz) chocolate, and the water in a heavy pan over low heat. Stir until melted, then cool slightly. Beat into the eggs in a bowl.

2 Add the flour and caster sugar and beat until smooth and well blended. Pour into the tins and bake for 25–30 minutes, or until a skewer in the centre comes out clean. Cool in tins on rack for 10 minutes, then turn out and leave to cool.

3 For the truffle mixture, melt 125g (4oz) chocolate (*Tip 52*). Cool slightly, then stir in icing sugar, rest of butter, and 4 tbsp cream and stir until smooth. For the glaze, melt remaining chocolate and cream over low heat until smooth.

4 Sandwich layers with half the truffle mixture. Spread glaze over top and sides of cake. Pipe rest of truffle around the bottom.

64 CHOCOLATE CHARLOTTE
Makes 6–8 slices

Ingredients
melted butter, for mould
250g (8oz) plain chocolate, chopped
175ml (6fl oz) strong black coffee
250g (8oz) unsalted butter, cut into pieces
200g (7oz) caster sugar
4 eggs
Decoration
125g (4oz) plain chocolate
1½ recipe quantities
Chantilly cream (Tip 94)
chocolate curls
(Tip 58)

2 △ Bring almost to the boil, stirring all the time, then remove from heat and whisk in eggs one by one. Strain into the mould. Bake until a thick crust forms on the surface, about 70 minutes. Leave to cool in the mould on a rack.

1 △ Brush a 1 litre (1⅔ pint) mould with melted butter and line and butter base. Preheat oven to 180°C/350°F/gas 4. Melt chocolate in heavy pan with coffee, stir until smooth, then add butter and sugar and stir well.

3 △ Cover and refrigerate for at least 24 hours. To unmould, run a knife around the edge to loosen the cake. Dip the base briefly into hot water and then invert over a plate to turn out. Remove paper and chill until ready to decorate.

4 △ Melt chocolate and spread evenly on strip of silicone paper. Leave until almost set. Cut circles with 4cm (1½in) cutter and leave to set. Turn over, peel off paper and lift off coins.

5 △ Spread a little Chantilly cream over the top of the charlotte. Place remainder in piping bag with medium star nozzle and pipe vertical lines to cover sides. Pipe swirls round base and top edge. Decorate with coins and curls.

TIMING
Decorate when almost ready to serve.

LITTLE CAKES

65 FAIRY-TALE HOUSES
Makes 2 small cakes

Ingredients
½ quantity Victoria sponge
mixture (Tip 28)
Decoration
4 tbsp apricot glaze
(Tip 87)
250g (8oz) sugar paste
(Tip 88)
food colourings
250g (8oz) icing sugar,
plus extra for dusting
1 egg white
chocolate sticks, or thins

TO SERVE
*For a children's party,
make several cakes and
arrange them in a row to
create a street of houses.*

1 Grease and line a 500g (1lb) loaf tin. Preheat oven to 160°C/325°F/gas 3.
2 Spoon mixture into tin and bake for 1 hour, or until a skewer comes out clean. Turn out onto a wire rack and leave to cool. Remove paper.
3 Cut the cake crosswise into 2 pieces. Slice off the corners from each cut end to make the roofs. Trim the other sides flat, making 2 cubes of 7cm (3in) with a roof shape on top. Brush with glaze.
4 Cut the sugar paste in half. Knead a different food colouring into each half. On a surface dusted with icing sugar, roll out each piece into a strip about 7 x 30cm (3 x 12in). Wrap neatly around the cubes and trim edges. Beat the icing sugar into the egg white until smooth. Place in a paper icing bag and snip a tiny piece off the end to make a very small hole. Pipe windows and a door on each cake. Stick chocolate "tiles" on top with glaze.

66 ALMOND BARS
Makes 15

Ingredients
125g (4oz) unsalted butter
125g (4oz) caster sugar
1 egg
1 tsp finely grated lemon zest
200g (7oz) plain flour, sifted with
1 tsp baking powder
Topping
100g (3½oz) butter
100g (3½oz) caster sugar
2 tbsp light soft brown sugar
2 tbsp milk
250g (8oz) flaked almonds

Buttery nut crunch tops light sponge

1 Grease and line a 23cm (9in) shallow, square tin. Preheat oven to 180°C/350°F/gas 4. For topping, melt butter and add sugars and milk. Bring to the boil, then remove from the heat and stir in almonds.
2 Beat butter and sugar until pale and fluffy. Beat in egg and lemon zest. Beat in flour until evenly mixed. Spoon mixture into tin and then spread topping over evenly.
3 Bake for 35 minutes or until just golden. Cut into bars while warm.

67 MADELEINES
Preheat oven to 230°C/450°F/gas 8. Grease and flour 25–30 medium madeleine moulds. Sift 125g (4oz) plain flour with 1 tsp baking powder. Whisk 4 eggs and 135g (4½ oz) caster sugar until the mixture is pale and thick and forms a ribbon trail (*Tip 19*). Beat in the grated zest of 1 orange.

Fold in the flour in 3 batches, adding 125g (4oz) melted butter with the last batch. Chill the batter for 25–30 minutes until it stiffens. Spoon the batter into the moulds so that they are two-thirds full.

TRADITIONAL MADELEINE SHAPE

Bake for 5 minutes, then reduce the heat to 200°C/ 400°F/gas 6 and bake until golden brown with a peak in the centre, 5–7 minutes. Turn out on to a rack to cool.

68 CHOUX PASTRY

Choux pastry cakes look hard to make, but are very quick and easy if you follow these step-by-step instructions.

Ingredients
125g (4oz) strong plain flour
pinch of salt
2 tsp caster sugar
100g (3½oz) butter
250ml (8fl oz) water
4 eggs, lightly beaten

1 △ Sift the flour, salt and sugar on to a piece of paper. Melt the butter in the water in a heavy-based pan, then bring to a fast, rolling boil. Remove from the heat and tip in the flour all at once.

Finished paste is thick and glossy

2 △ Beat in the flour, return the pan to a low heat, and beat rapidly until it forms a smooth and glossy paste that rolls cleanly off the sides of the pan. Allow to cool for 5 minutes, then begin to beat in the egg a little at a time.

3 ▷ Continue adding beaten egg until the mixture is smooth and glossy, then gradually add more until the paste falls heavily from the spoon (you may not need all the egg).

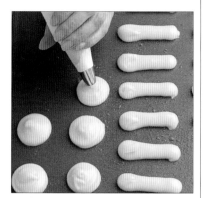

4 △ To make puffs or éclairs, spoon into piping bag with plain 1cm (½in) nozzle. Pipe on to greased baking sheet. Brush with egg. Preheat oven to 220°C/425°F/gas 7. Bake for 15–20 minutes.

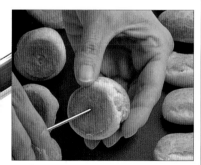

5 △ Pierce the base of each puff with a skewer to release steam, then bake for another 5 minutes until firm and golden brown. Cool on a wire rack.

USEFUL WATCHPOINTS
Run the greased baking sheet under cold water so it is slightly wet. Pipe the puffs well apart on the sheet, as they spread.

69 ÉCLAIRS
Makes 12

Ingredients
1 recipe quantity choux pastry (Tip 68)
Filling and decoration
90ml (3fl oz) double cream
1 recipe quantity pastry cream (Tip 93)
125g (4oz) chocolate, melted (Tip 52)

1 Preheat the oven to 220°C/425°F/gas 7. Pipe the choux pastry as shown, making 12 lines 10cm (4in) long and 5cm (2in) apart. Brush with leftover beaten egg.
2 Bake for 20 minutes, then pierce the base of each one (*Step 5, left*). Bake for 3–5 minutes until crisp and golden. Cool on a wire rack.
3 Slice each éclair in half. Whip the cream stiffly, then fold into the pastry cream. Spoon into a piping bag with a 1cm (½in) nozzle and pipe onto the bottom half of each éclair. Cover with the top.
4 Leave the melted chocolate until thick. Spread the top of each éclair with chocolate and leave until set.

Éclairs are best eaten the same day

TOPPINGS & FILLINGS

70 VERSATILE VARIETY

The large variety of cake toppings ranges from marble-smooth sugar paste or royal icing to soft toppings like glacé icing, butter cream, whipped cream, and whipped frostings. Many toppings can be used as fillings, making them very versatile.

MOCHA CREAM FILLING

71 BUTTER CREAM & VARIATIONS

Makes enough to fill and cover a 20cm (8in) Victoria sponge

Ingredients
125g (4oz) unsalted butter, softened
250g (8oz) icing sugar, sifted
1 tsp vanilla extract
1 tbsp milk or cream

Spread with a palette knife

Place the butter in a bowl and gradually beat in the sugar until the mixture is pale and creamy. Add vanilla, then beat in milk or cream for a spreading consistency.

Variations

Chocolate: Melt 100g (3½oz) plain chocolate. Cool, then beat in.

Coffee: Dissolve 2 tbsp instant coffee powder in 1 tbsp boiling water. Cool, then beat in.

Lemon: Beat in 1 tbsp fresh lemon juice and finely grated zest of 1 large lemon.

Orange: Beat in 1 tbsp fresh orange juice and finely grated zest of 1 large orange.

72 COATING A CAKE WITH BUTTER CREAM

Spread the butter cream in a generous, even layer over the top and sides, using a palette knife. The sides can be marked with horizontal lines using a confectionery comb. Hold the comb vertically, and drag quickly but firmly through the cream.

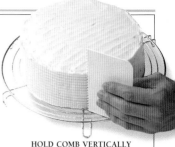

HOLD COMB VERTICALLY

APPLY COATING WITH A PALETTE KNIFE

73 DECORATING THE SIDES OF A CAKE

After covering, the sides of a cake can be coated with grated chocolate or chopped nuts. Balance the cake on the palm of one hand over the plate of coating. Lift the coating on to the sides of the cake with a palette knife, pressing gently so it stays in place.

74 MOUSSELINE BUTTER CREAM

This firm and smooth butter cream will hold its shape even in warm weather. To ensure it spreads easily, bring the cream back to room temperature before using. It can be frozen for up to 1 month.

1 Gently melt 75g (2½oz) granulated sugar in 4 tbsp water then boil to 115°C/240°F on a sugar thermometer.

2 Whisk 3 egg yolks, then gradually whisk in the hot sugar syrup. Whisk for 5 minutes until pale and thick.

3 Cream 175g (6oz) soft butter and beat in the egg mixture gradually. Flavour with vanilla, then chill for 30 minutes.

75 FILLING A PIPING BAG

Use a nylon piping bag, or make one from a triangle of greaseproof paper. Drop a nozzle into the bag, then carefully push it right down to the end. Fold back the bag's top and half-fill, pushing down to remove air pockets. Unfold top; twist tightly just above filling. Hold twisted top and pipe.

FOLD OVER TOP AND FILL BAG

76 BUTTER CREAM DECORATIONS

A nylon piping bag with a nozzle is best for butter cream (and whipped cream). Hold bag upright with top twisted and squeeze from top of piping bag with firm, even pressure, retwisting as it empties.

STORAGE
Store butter cream in a covered container in the refrigerator until needed.

NOZZLES ▽
For many designs you just need a 1cm (½in) star nozzle.

△ STAR

△ RIBBON

△ SMALL STAR

ROSETTES △
Use 1cm (½in) star nozzle. A circular motion forms a swirl with a peak.

SMALL STARS △
Use 1.25mm (1/16in) nozzle. Hold bag upright. Squeeze out without twisting bag.

OVERLAPPING SHELLS △
Use 1cm (½in) star nozzle. Hold bag at 95° angle towards you. Pipe briefly away from you, then curl icing back over and down on itself. Start next one in front of tip of last one.

LONG ROPE △
Use 1cm (½in) star nozzle. Hold bag at 95° angle towards you. Pipe in a continuous movement, twisting the icing into a tight spiral. A ribbon nozzle gives a flat rope.

77 WHIPPED FROSTINGS

Make boiled sugar syrup (*Tip 10*), and boil until it reaches 120°C/248°F. Beat 4 egg whites until stiff, then gradually add syrup, beating constantly, until it is fluffy and holds peaks. Spread while warm.

78 AMERICAN FUDGE FROSTING

Melt 60g (2oz) chocolate, 300g (10oz) sugar, 125ml (4fl oz) milk, 60g (2oz) butter, 1 tbsp golden syrup, and a pinch of salt in a heavy pan. Boil for 1 minute, stirring. Cool, then beat until thick.

79 COATING WITH WHIPPED FROSTING

Whipped frosting sets on standing, so it must be spread in swirls and peaks while still warm.

If frosting is too thin, whisk over hot water until stiff. If it sets too fast, add 1–2 tsp boiling water.

1 Coat both the top and the sides of the cake generously with frosting while it is still warm.

2 Using a metal spatula, swirl up the frosting, pulling it into soft peaks evenly over the cake top.

3 Go on swirling until the top is decorated all over, then repeat the swirling around the sides.

80 CREAM CHEESE FROSTING

Place 125g (4oz) cream cheese in a bowl. Sift in 15g (½oz) icing sugar and beat until the mixture is smooth. Reserve 1½ tbsp from 150ml (¼ pint) double cream, then gradually beat in the remainder until the frosting has a soft dropping consistency. Do not overbeat – the frosting thickens as it is spread. If necessary, thin down the frosting with the reserved cream.

A FROSTED LAYER CAKE

55

81 GLACÉ ICING

Sift 200g (7oz) icing sugar into a bowl (for chocolate glacé replace 30g (1oz) of sugar with cocoa powder). Gradually stir in 7–8 tbsp boiling water until icing is smooth and coats the back of a spoon. Rest bowl over simmering water until warm. Use at once.

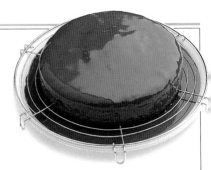

STAND THE CAKE ON A RACK TO ICE

Pour icing on to centre of cake

82 APPLYING GLACÉ ICING

Stand the cake on a rack and brush with warm apricot glaze (*Tip 87*). Leave 5 minutes. Warm the icing until thick enough to coat a spoon; beat in sifted icing sugar if it is too thin. Pour over the cake so that it drips down the sides. Immediately, take a metal spatula dipped in hot water to warm it and use to spread the top and then the sides smooth.

83 RICH GLACÉ ICING

This is the classic icing for the rich chocolate cake, Sachertorte, and is excellent for covering any cakes. Pour 200ml (7fl oz) double cream into a pan, place over low heat and bring slowly to the boil. Remove from the heat and stir in 150g (5oz) finely grated plain chocolate until melted. Leave to cool and thicken a little, but pour on while still warm and liquid. Tilt rack until cake is covered in an even layer.

EXTRA DECORATION
Cover the top with chocolate scrolls (Tip 57) and dust with icing sugar.

56

84 FEATHERED ICING

An attractive feathered effect can be created by piping chocolate or other contrasting icing on top of butter cream or glacé icing. Use either a small paper cone, or a piping bag fitted with a writing nozzle.

1 ◁ Coat the cake with icing. Make a paper cone from a square of greaseproof paper and fill with melted chocolate. Cut off the tip of the cone to make a 3mm (⅛in) hole. Starting right at the centre and moving out to the edge, pipe concentric circles on top of the cake.

2 ◁ Before chocolate hardens, quickly draw lines like spokes about 4cm (1½in) apart using a cocktail stick or the tip of a small knife. Alternate the direction of each spoke, working first from edge to centre, then from centre to edge.

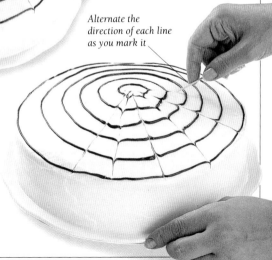

Alternate the direction of each line as you mark it

3 ▷ Go on all around the top of the cake, alternating each spoke, until it is evenly covered with the feathered design.

ANOTHER METHOD
Pipe the icing in one continuous spiral, from the centre out. Make the spokes as detailed above.

85 MARZIPAN

Marzipan (almond paste) is used both as a cake covering on its own, and as a base for icing. Rich fruit cakes that are to be covered with sugar paste (*Tip 88*) or royal icing (*Tip 90*) need first to have a layer of marzipan, to prevent the icing becoming discoloured. If the top of the cake is not flat, start by levelling it with a separate circle of marzipan. Try making your own (*Tip 86*); it will be vastly superior to the shop-bought varieties.

1 △ Brush the cake with apricot glaze (Tip 87). To level the top of a 20cm (8in) cake, evenly roll out 250g (8oz) marzipan to a circle just larger than the diameter of the cake. Invert the cake on to it and trim and neaten the edges.

2 △ Turn the cake right side up and place on a cake board. To cover the whole cake with marzipan, measure across the top and down the sides with a piece of string. This measurement is the diameter of the circle of marzipan required to cover the cake.

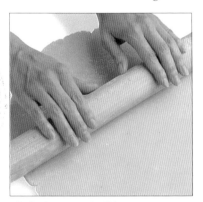

3 △ Place 750g (1½lb) marzipan on a surface lightly dusted with icing sugar. Using a long, straight-ended rolling pin, roll out the marzipan into a large circle of even thickness, using the string as a guide to the diameter. Brush off any excess icing sugar.

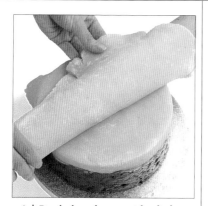

4 △ Brush the cake top with a little brandy. Using the rolling pin, lift the circle of marzipan and unroll over the cake. Press the marzipan smoothly on to the sides and top of the cake, using your fingers to mould it to shape.

5 △ Trim off excess marzipan at the base. Leave to dry in a cool place for at least 24 hours before applying sugar paste or royal icing. Before covering the cake with sugar paste, you can brush the marzipan surface with a little more brandy, for added flavour.

86 HOME-MADE MARZIPAN
Makes about 500g (1lb)

Ingredients
125g (4oz) icing sugar, sifted
125g (4oz) caster sugar, sifted
250g (8oz) ground almonds
1 tsp lemon juice
few drops of almond extract
2 egg whites

1 Mix the sugars and the ground almonds in a bowl. Add lemon juice, almond extract, and enough egg white to make a soft dough.
2 Knead briefly on a surface dusted with icing sugar until smooth. Wrap in clingfilm and keep in a cool place until ready to use.

MARZIPAN-COVERED FRUIT & LAYER CAKES

87 APRICOT GLAZE
Heat 125g (4oz) apricot jam and 3 tbsp cold water together in a small pan until the jam has melted. Strain into a small bowl, pressing with a wooden spoon. Warm the glaze again before using.

88 SUGAR PASTE

Also known as fondant icing, sugar paste is used to ice novelty cakes and wedding cakes. It gives a very smooth, professional finish. This recipe makes enough to cover a 20cm (8in) cake.

Mix with a knife

1 Sift 425g (14oz) icing sugar into a bowl. Add 1 egg white and 1 tbsp liquid glucose, and stir with a small round-bladed knife until it starts to come together in clumps.
2 Knead to form a ball, then turn out onto a surface lightly dusted with icing sugar. Knead for about 10 minutes, or until very smooth. Dust with icing sugar to prevent it sticking. Wrap tightly in clingfilm.

89 APPLYING SUGAR PASTE

Rich fruit cakes must be covered with marzipan (*Tip 85*) before applying sugar paste, to prevent the fruit staining the icing.

For sponge cakes, brush first with apricot glaze (*Tip 87*). After rolling, lay the paste over the cake quickly, before it stretches out of shape.

1 Measure the cake (*Tip 85*). Roll out the paste into a large circle on a surface dusted with icing sugar. Gently bring the far edge over the rolling pin towards you.

2 Carefully lift the sugar paste on the pin. With the end nearest you touching the cake board, drape it over the cake and let it fall neatly down the other side.

3 Smooth over the top and sides of the cake. Dip your fingers in icing sugar and smooth away any creases. Trim off excess paste at the base with a small sharp knife.

90 ROYAL ICING

For a 23cm (9in) cake, sift 500g (1lb) icing sugar. Beat 2 egg whites until frothy and beat in the sugar 1 tbsp at a time. Beat in 1 tsp lemon juice, then beat for 8–10 minutes until soft peaks form. Use at once, or cover the bowl with a wet cloth until ready to use.

91 APPLYING ROYAL ICING

Cover the cake with marzipan (*Tip 85*), then spoon on the icing. Using a paddling motion, work it evenly over the cake and down the sides with a palette knife. Draw a metal spatula across the cake to smooth the surface and neaten the edges.

92 PIPING WHIPPED CREAM

Choose either double or whipping cream. Whip until stiff peaks form, but don't overbeat or the cream will become granular. Spoon into a piping bag with a large star nozzle to make scrolls, stars, or shells.

USE A STAR NOZZLE TO MAKE DIFFERENT DESIGNS

93 PASTRY CREAM

Bring 275ml (9fl oz) milk to the boil. Beat 3 egg yolks and 60g (2oz) caster sugar in a bowl until pale and creamy. Sift in 15g (½oz) flour and 15g (½oz) cornflour and beat until smooth. Pour the hot milk onto the egg mixture and mix well. Return to the pan and bring to the boil, stirring well. Simmer for 2 minutes, beating all the time, until smooth and thick. Stir in ½ tsp vanilla extract and 3 tbsp double cream. Pour into a bowl

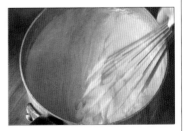

BEAT UNTIL VERY SMOOTH

and press clingfilm or buttered greaseproof paper onto the surface to prevent a skin forming. Cool, then chill for 2 hours before using.

94 CHANTILLY CREAM

Chantilly cream is double cream whipped with sugar and flavoured with vanilla, brandy, rum – or a liqueur such as Grand Marnier. It is used for filling and decorating cakes, or you can pipe it to form rosettes or other decorations.

Chill a bowl and place it inside a larger bowl half full of iced water. Place 250ml (8fl oz) double cream in the bowl. Whip until it forms soft peaks. Add 1 tbsp caster sugar and ½ tsp vanilla extract or 1 tsp other flavouring. Whip until it forms soft peaks again and just holds its shape.

The cream will soften slightly when sugar is added

BEWARE OF OVERBEATING
Be careful not to overbeat the cream until it looks granular, because it will then separate and turn into butter.

95 WALNUT CAKE
Makes 8 slices

Ingredients
250g (8oz) plain chocolate
250g (8oz) walnut pieces
125g (4oz) unsalted butter
200g (7oz) caster sugar
4 eggs, separated
250ml (8fl oz) Chantilly cream (Tip 94)
chocolate leaves (Tip 59)

1 △ Grease and then line a 23cm (9in) springform tin. Preheat the oven to 150°C/300°F/gas 2. Chop 200g (7oz) of the chocolate. Grind with the walnuts in a food processor (do this in 2 batches). Cream the butter, add three-quarters of the sugar, and beat until light and fluffy. Add the egg yolks one by one, beating well again after each addition. Stir the chocolate and walnut mixture into the creamed mixture using a rubber spatula.

2 △ Whisk the egg whites until stiff. Sprinkle in the remaining sugar and whisk until glossy. Add this to the chocolate mixture and fold together using a rubber spatula. Spoon into the tin and smooth the top with the spatula.

3 △ Bake until a skewer inserted into the centre comes out clean, 60–70 minutes. Allow to cool completely in the tin. When cold, release the clips and lift the sides away from the cake. Leave the cake sitting on the tin base.

4 △ With a palette knife, spread the Chantilly cream evenly over the top and sides of the cake. Place on a serving plate and chill for 1 hour. Chop the remaining chocolate and melt in a bowl over a pan of hot water. Spoon into a piping bag fitted with a writing nozzle, or a paper cone, and pipe lightly over the top of the cake. Decorate the base of the cake around the serving plate with chocolate leaves.

The cake is delicate, so do not remove cake tin base

96 GÂTEAU ST HONORÉ
Makes 6–8 slices

Ingredients
250g (8oz) prepared sweet
shortcrust pastry
1 quantity choux pastry
(Tip 68), made with
125ml (4fl oz) each milk
and water
leftover beaten egg from
choux pastry
1 egg yolk
200g (7oz) granulated
sugar
3 tbsp water
Filling
150ml (¼ pint) double
cream
2 tsp caster sugar
2 quantities pastry cream
(Tip 93)

1 Roll out the sweet pastry on a lightly floured surface into a 23cm (9in) circle. Place on a greased baking sheet, prick with a fork, and chill. Preheat the oven to 200°C/400°F/gas 6.
2 Spoon the choux pastry into a piping bag with a plain 1cm (½in) nozzle. Mix the leftover beaten egg with the egg yolk and use a little to brush a 2.5cm (1in) strip round the edge of the pastry circle. Pipe choux pastry in a raised thick band around the outside edge of the pastry.
3 Pipe the remaining choux pastry into 12–14 small balls on a wetted baking sheet. Brush the puffs and choux ring with the egg. Bake the choux puffs (*Tip 68*) and cool on a wire rack.
4 Bake the pastry base for 10 minutes, then lower the heat to 190°C/375°F/gas 5 and bake for another 20 minutes, or until the pastry and choux ring are golden brown. Prick the choux pastry to release steam, then return to the oven

GLAZING, FILLING, & ATTACHING THE CHOUX PUFFS

1 Spear each choux puff with the tip of a sharp knife. Dip the top into the caramel and leave to set on a wire rack.

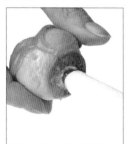

2 Pipe whipped cream into each choux puff through the steam hole in the base until the puff feels firm and full.

3 Quickly dip the base of each puff into the caramel and arrange side by side around the top of the choux ring.

for 5 minutes. Leave on a wire rack to cool.
5 Melt sugar and water in a pan, then boil for about 7 minutes until it reaches 173°C/345°F on a sugar thermometer. Plunge base of pan into cold water. Glaze the choux puffs (*see left*).
6 Whip the cream and sugar into stiff peaks. Spoon into a piping bag with a 5mm (¼in) nozzle. Pipe cream into each puff and dip bases in caramel (*see left*). Arrange around top of ring.
7 Spoon pastry cream into a piping bag with a 1cm (½in) star nozzle and pipe into the centre of the ring. Chill for 1 hour before serving.

GETTING ORGANIZED
Make the pastry cream the day before. Make the choux pastry a few hours ahead, then cover closely and refrigerate. To keep the caramel liquid while glazing and attaching the puffs, stand the pan in a bowl of very hot water.

Pastry cream is piped into a decorative rope design

MAKING DECORATIONS

97 MARZIPAN FRUIT & LEAVES

Use shop-bought marzipan, or (even better) make your own (*Tip 86*). Knead a small amount until it is soft and pliable. To tint, sprinkle on a few drops of food colouring, then knead in well. Roll or just mould with your hands to form fruit or leaf shapes. Use a small sharp knife to make details or to cut out leaves.

△ TOUCH OF REALISM
Quite realistic details can be moulded onto the fruit with a special plastic tool.

MAKING HOLLY LEAVES

1 Tint the marzipan green with food colouring and roll out thinly on a surface dusted with icing sugar. Cut into diamond shapes with a small sharp knife.

2 Using a small pastry cutter or the tip of a small knife, cut a series of curves out of the edges of the shapes to form leaves. Alternatively, use a leaf-shaped cutter.

3 Mould the holly leaves to form pointed tips. Add holly berries, if liked, by rolling marzipan, tinted red, into small balls. Leave to dry before placing on the cake.

98 ROYAL ICING DECORATIONS

Royal icing (*Tip 90*) holds a stiff, crisp shape that makes it ideal for ribbons, roses, lattice, and scrolls. They can be white, or delicately tinted to show up against a white icing background. Complicated designs are best done in stages to allow the icing to dry.
Keep bowl of icing covered with a wet cloth.

△ **Double-sided shells**: *use an 8-point star nozzle to pipe a row and another by its side.*

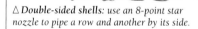

6-POINT STAR	RIBBON/PETAL

4-POINT STAR	FINE WRITING NOZZLE

△ **Roses and leaves**: *use a petal nozzle for roses and leaves and a fine nozzle for links.*

△ **Scrolls and rosettes**: *use a 6-point star nozzle to pipe scrolls and small rosettes.*

△ **Long-tailed shell design**: *use an 8-point star nozzle to pipe a lattice in a shell design.*

△ **Lattice**: *use a 6-point star nozzle to pipe shells, and a writing nozzle for the lines.*

△ **Swirls**: *use a 4-point star nozzle for swirls, and a writing nozzle for dots and lines.*

△ **Rosettes and stars**: *use a 4-point star nozzle to pipe a chain of rosettes and small stars.*

△ **Basket weave**: *use a ribbon nozzle to make a series of strips, and a fine nozzle to link them.*

99 SUGAR-FROSTED FLOWERS & FRUIT

Sugar-frosted flowers and fruit make very attractive cake decorations for a special occasion. Flowers should be prepared as near to serving time as possible. Choose edible ones such as roses, nasturtiums, or violets – preferably homegrown and not sprayed with chemicals. Select flowers with strong stems and thick petals and keep in water in a cool place. Fruit such as bunches of grapes or strawberries can be prepared a few hours in advance of when you will need it.

△ FROSTING FLOWERS
Cut off the flower head, leaving a small stem. Coat each petal evenly with a thin layer of lightly beaten egg white, using a small paintbrush. Spoon a little caster sugar between each petal to coat well, then shake out excess. Push stems through a wire rack. Leave to dry.

◁ FROSTING FRUIT
Separate the fruit or keep in small bunches. Lightly whisk 2 egg whites and sift caster sugar onto a plate. Dip each piece of fruit into the egg white, then spoon on the caster sugar until evenly coated. Transfer to a wire rack to dry.

100 CHERRIES IN CHOCOLATE

Chocolate-coated cherries are a traditional decoration for cakes such as Black Forest cake (*Tip 41*). Melt 30g (1oz) plain chocolate in a small bowl over hot water (*Tip 52*). Select perfect black cherries with stems. Holding the cherries by their stems, dip each one into the chocolate to coat evenly. Place on silicone paper and leave to set.

HOLD EACH CHERRY BY THE STEM TO DIP

101 CHOCOLATE COCONUT CAKE
Makes 8 slices

Inner skin left on coconut edges gives definition and colour contrast

Ingredients
cocoa powder
90g (3oz) plain chocolate
250g (8oz) self-raising flour
30g (10oz) caster sugar
300ml (½ pint) buttermilk
125g (4oz) butter, softened
½ tsp baking powder
3 eggs
100g (3½oz) desiccated coconut
chocolate butter cream (Tip 71)
300ml (½ pint) double cream, whipped stiffly
coconut ruffles, to decorate

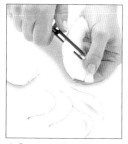

△ **COCONUT RUFFLES**
Break open a fresh coconut and prise out pieces of meat. Draw the blade of a vegetable peeler down the curved edges of the coconut pieces to make paper-thin ruffles with an attractive dark contrasting edge.

1 Preheat oven to 180°C/350°F/gas 4. Grease 2 x 23cm (9in) round tins and dust with cocoa.
2 Melt chocolate (*Tip 52*). Place the flour, sugar, buttermilk, butter, baking powder, and eggs in a food processor with the chocolate. Beat until well mixed, scraping down sides with rubber spatula. Beat for 2 minutes, then stir in coconut.
3 Spread mixture evenly in the tins. Bake for 35 minutes, or until skewer in centre comes out clean. Cool in tins on wire rack for 10 minutes, then turn out and leave to cool completely.
4 Cut each cake horizontally into 2 layers. Place 1 layer on a serving plate and spread with half the butter cream. Cover with second layer. Spread with half the whipped cream. Cover with another cake layer and spread with remaining butter cream. Top with last cake layer and spread with remaining cream. Decorate with ruffles and sieve cocoa powder over centre.

INDEX

ACKNOWLEDGMENTS

Dorling Kindersley would like to thank Hilary Bird for compiling the index, Fiona Wild for proof-reading and editorial help, and Robert Campbell and Mark Bracey for DTP assistance.

Photography
All photographs by Martin Brigdale, Martin Cameron, Andy Crawford, Dave King, Terry McCormick, David Murray, Jules Selmes, and Jerry Young.

Additional recipes & techniques
Recipes and techniques by Anne Willan: Tip 21 *Genoese cake*; Tip 23 *Angel food cake*; Tip 41 *Black Forest cake*; Tip 64 *Chocolate charlotte*; Tip 67 *Madeleines*; Tip 77 *Whipped frostings*; Tip 78 *American fudge frosting*; Tip 86 *Home-made marzipan*; Tip 90 *Royal icing*; Tip 94 *Chantilly cream*; Tip 95 *Walnut cake*. Recipes and techniques copyright © 1991 Dorling Kindersley and The Hearst Corporation. Reprinted from *The Good Housekeeping Illustrated Book of Desserts* by arrangement with William Morrow & Company, Inc., a division of The Hearst Corporation: Tip 40 *Lattice-top cappuccino cake*; Tip 46 *Pavlova*; Tip 63 *Chocolate truffle cake*; Tip 84 *Feathered icing*; Tip 101 *Chocolate coconut cake*.